DEBBIEDOO'S

home

PRESSURE COOKING

Taking the stress out of pressure

COOKBOOK

Contents

2	Introduction
3	The Pressure Cooker
4	Glossary
5	Soups
17	Sides
26	Pastas
35	Beef
50	Pork
55	Chicken
68	Holiday Treats
74	Desserts
89	Connect With Debbiedoo

Introduction

What exactly is a home pressure cooker, and why do you need one? After all, your crockpot has been just fine all these years. The Instant Pot electric pressure cooker has been around since 2010, but really became the buzz during the last six months of 2016.

First, let me explain what a pressure cooker is. Pressure cooking is the process of cooking food, using water, broth or other cooking liquids. Heck, beer and wine work well too! The cooking process is in a sealed vessel, known as a pressure cooker. Pressure cookers cook food not only faster than conventional cooking methods, but they also lock in the flavor and juices better than no other. It saves you time, energy (literally), and saves you the everyday hassle of wondering what's for dinner tonight.

The pressure from the cooker is created by boiling a liquid, such as water or broth, inside the closed pressure cooker. The trapped steam increases the internal pressure and allows the temperature to rise. After use, the pressure is slowly released so that the vessel can be safely opened. Some pots feature a quick release option as well.

Almost any food that can be cooked in your oven can be pressure cooked. Cooking time is greatly reduced as foods cook up to 70% faster when a pressure cooker is used, making it a handy tool to quickly get the meal on the table.

Meet Debbiedoo

Hi, I'm Debbie! You may have seen me in my weekly live cooking videos where I share tips and tricks of the pot. I have to confess, I have never been one to LOVE cookin' in the kitchen. I think I disliked the clean up more than anything. Fortunately, I have a husband and family who helped with that aspect of it. Regardless, why do we want to spend extra time cleaning off greasy stoves, wiping down counters and then cleaning 3 pots? We don't! Surely there are better things to do with our time.

Hence, the Instant Pot was born. I fell in love immediately. One would think the husband would get jealous of a new love connection. However, this pot has brought us closer because I truly believe the way to a man's heart is through his stomach. My husband and family are getting more home cooked meals than they have in the past 20 years! No kidding. That only means more love my way :) A happy wife makes a happy life!

My goal is to help you use your pressure cooker to fall in love with cooking and bring your family closer together too! I've packed this book with some of my favorite pressure cooker recipes to get you started on easy dinners, holidays dishes, and even healthy Weight Watcher meals!

The Pressure Cooker

What's the difference between a crockpot and a pressure cooker? Let's clarify:

Pressure cookers are built like ordinary pots and pans except their lids are fashioned to close and lock tightly in place, creating a seal that traps steam inside the pot. Unable to escape, the steam builds up pressure, raising the temperature inside, which causes food to cook about 70% faster than conventional stovetop cooking. The steam also helps keep food juicy along with the added liquid of choice. Back in Grandma's day, pressure cookers were built to be used on your stovetop. However, modern day models can simply be placed on a countertop and plugged in for power.

Slow cookers cook food anywhere from 4 to 10 hours. They are never used on the stovetop and once you load your ingredients and plug them in, you can safely leave them unattended so your food can cook overnight while you sleep or while you're out of the house during the day. Long, slow cooking yields tender, falling off the bone meats and poultry, making slow cookers a perfect cooking method for inexpensive cuts of meat which are usually tough. Another slow cooker convenience is the ability to safely and easily transport food. Although for me personally I never found that convenient. I used to have to duct tape the lid to stay on, unlike the pressure cooker where the lid is securely locked into place.

With today's modern pressure cooker, there are many options now to cook per the meal or dessert you are preparing. Did I mention my new pot even has a sauté option, which means no extra clean up in the kitchen before throwing my meal in? One pot, one clean up. YAHOO!

Why I fell in LOVE with my new pot, which by the way is my one and only addiction-- It literally has changed my life and attitude toward preparing meals for our family every night.

Here's the biggest difference between a slow cooker and a pressure cooker: One is slow, and one is fast. With a pressure cooker, you can be unprepared until 6:00 p.m., when you come home from work all frantic as to what you are going to cook. You can pull a nice cut of beef, pork or chicken and have dinner from prep to table in an hour or less (in most cases).

My experience has been that the pressure cooker deals with vegetables much better than the slow cooker, which tends to make them mushy.

Most serving sizes in this book are between 4-6. Please note, this book does not include nutrition or calorie facts. Any pressure cooker brand will work accordingly to these recipes. I just happen to have the IP (Instant Pot).

Glossary

If you are new to the Instant Pot community, please get familiar with some basic terms outlined below that you will see time and again in the pressure cooking circles. Read the manual before first use. You must clean your inner pot and lid first and be sure to do the required water test.

Sealing Ring – The silicone ring that sits inside the lid. This is what seals the pot. If it is not properly installed in place, your food will not cook properly. Some suggest buying an extra sealing ring for smelly foods like garlic or fish. The silicone does hold on to odors of food--that sort of drives me nuts! I would also recommend a different silicone ring for desserts. Who wants your cheesecake to smell like pot roast?? Not me!

Pressure Valve – The black valve on the top of the lid that seals or releases pressure. There are two settings for it: 1. Sealing (pressure) and 2. Venting (slow cooking or releasing pressure). Important functions and buttons on your Pressure Cooker.

Your Instant Pot is well designed and the buttons on it will help you cook your food better. So, the sensors that know how to heat certain food will even help not to burn or overcook the food you're trying to serve up.

While it's not foolproof, you're still in control of the time and even if you send it through another cycle, it's got so many wonderful safety features and programmed cooking features.

Keep Warm/Cancel – This will cancel any program that has been set and puts the cooker in standby. When the cooker is in standby, pressing this key will activate the keep-warm program and can last to almost 100 hours.

Soup – This is for making various soups or broths. The default for this setting is high pressure for 30 minutes. This can be adjusted with the ADJUST or plus and minus buttons.

Porridge – This is for making porridge or oatmeal of various grains. The default for this setting is high pressure for 20 minutes. **DO NOT use quick release for this setting, it will result in a mess** This setting should only be used with the pressure valve set to SEALING.

Instant Pot Terms

IP – Instant Pot

HP – High Pressure

LP – Low Pressure

QR – Quick Release – This means you are releasing the pressure by turning the pressure valve to the open position immediately after food is finished cooking.

There will be hot steam coming out of the top, so make sure your hand isn't covering the opening… and that you don't scare yourself! I've jumped ☺ But did not burn myself, thankfully.

NPR – Natural Pressure Release – This allows the pressure to come down on its own without releasing the valve and takes a little bit of time. It will also vary based on if you have a 6 quart or 8-quart pressure cooker.

PIP – Pot in Pot – This means using another container inside of your Instant Pot. Since the Instant Pot does not get as hot during pressure cooking (up to 248°F) as ovens while baking, you can use any oven-proof container such as glass, stainless steel, or silicone cups or molds that fit in the pressure cooker.

Soups

6	Beef Brisket Chili
7	Chicken Noodle Soup with Pastina
8	Chicken Tortellini Soup
9	Endive & Arugula Soup
10	Hamburger Ginger Noodle Soup
11	Pumpkin Soup
12	Taco Soup
13	Weight Watchers Friendly Tuscan Soup
14	Weight Watchers Friendly Vegetable Soup
15	White Bean Chicken Chili
16	Weight Watchers Friendly White Bean Chicken Chili

DEBBIEDOO'S

Beef Brisket Chili

Ingredients

3 tbsp All purpose flour
2 tbsp Ancho chile powder
1 tbsp Kosher salt
2 lbs Beef brisket
15 oz can Black beans
15 oz can Fire roasted diced tomatoes
1 Red bell pepper
1 Red onion
3 cloves Garlic minced
¾ cup Beef broth
4 tbsp olive oil
1 tbsp Cumin
1 tsp Dried oregeno

Directions

Combine meat, flour, chile powder, cumin, salt and oregano. Mix well.

Set pot to saute mode and add olive oil in the inner pot. Add the above mixed ingredients and lightly saute until meat is lightly brown. Be sure to stir as you saute.

Add beef broth, beans, tomatoes, onion, pepper and garlic to the pot.

Set pot to manual 35 minutes. Let the pot naturally release. Enjoy!

DEBBIEDOO'S
Chicken Noodle Soup
With Pastina

Ingredients

4 lb cooked Rotisserie chicken
½ can Cream of Chicken herb soup
½ can Cream of celery soup
32-oz. box Chicken stock
1½ cups Water
1 small bag Organic baby, mixed colored carrots
1 bunch Green scallions
Salt and Pepper to taste
2 cups Pastina

Directions

First, turn on your pressure cooker to saute mode and add in the box of chicken stock. While that starts simmering add the pre-shredded rotisserie chicken, carrots, scallions, and half a can of each soup flavor.

Add water. Mix all the ingredients well. Add salt and pepper to taste. Add 2 cups of pastina and mix well into the soup.

Set your pot to manual for 6 minutes. Close lid, hit seal. When it beeps, do a quick release, which in addition will take another few minutes.

Soup is on. Add a sprig or two of fresh parsley if desired.

This soup needs to cool off a bit before you dig in. It's so delicious!

DEBBIEDOO'S
Chicken Tortellini Soup

Ingredients

2½ cups Kale
(You may substitute spinach)
2½ tbsp Insta-Chicken
seasoning
1 box 32 oz Chicken broth
1½ cups mini carrots, halved
Pepper to taste
9 oz Three Cheese tortellini
2 cups Water

Directions

Turn pot on saute mode. Add broth, water, carrots, seasoning and chicken.

Let simmer low for 10 minutes. If you have a tempered glass lid, set pot on medium and put the lid on.

Add tortellini and mix. Place pressure cooker lid on bot and set for 4 minutes on High Pressure.

Do a quick release. Ready to serve with a piece of crusty bread. Enjoy!

DEBBIEDOO'S

Endive & Arugula Soup

Ingredients

3 cups Arugula
3 cups Endive
2 tbsp Garlic
32 oz Chicken stock
Turkey pepperoni to taste
2 cans (16 oz each) White
cannellini beans
Pepper to taste
Red pepper flake to taste
Olive oil

Directions

First set your pot to saute high mode. Drizzle in lightly on the bottom olive oil. Once that is warmed up, add in your Endive and saute a minute. Add in your Arugula, saute a minute.

Place tempered glass lid on for about 3-4 minutes and let the natural liquid from the greens deplete in the pot.

Remove lid and add in turkey pepperoni. Saute and mix well together.

Add in Chicken stock, cannellini beans and juice. Mix well and place lid back on for about 25 minutes on medium setting. You can peek and stir as you go along.

Add a little red pepper flake to taste and cut up some yummy crusty Italian bread. Enjoy! This is a keeper.

DEBBIEDOO'S
Hamburger Ginger Noodle Soup

Ingredients

2 lbs Lean ground beef
32 oz vegetable broth
Fresh ginger root
4 oz or ½ cup Ramen noodles
(found at local grocer in Asian section)
Salt and Pepper to taste

Optional:
Broccoli

Directions

Saute ground beef until brown. Add salt and pepper to taste while sauteing.

Drain grease if you are not using a lean beef.

Add approximately 2 tablespoons of freshly chopped ginger root to ground hamburger. (If using ground ginger, use 1½ tablespoons.) Stir well.

Add 32 oz of vegetable broth and 1 cup of water to the mixture. Set the pot on High Pressure Manual for 15 minutes.

Quick release and add noodles, cover in broth, and broccoli. Set the pot to High Pressure for 1 to 2 minutes.

Serve warm and enjoy!

DEBBIEDOO'S
Pumpkin Soup

Ingredients

2 Pumpkin pie pumpkins
13.5 oz can Coconut milk
1 tbsp Ground ginger
1 tbsp Ground turmeric
1 tbsp Curry powder
2½ cups Vegetable stock
Salt and Pepper to taste
1 cup water

Directions

Remove stem off of pumpkins. Add one cup of water to your pot. Place pumpkin on trivet and set the pot to High Pressure Manual for 13 minutes.

Natural release (10 minutes) and let pumpkin cool down. Repeat this same method for the second pumpkin. Cut pumpkins in half and remove the seeds and guts of the pumpkin. Remove the skin. It should peel right off perfectly.

In a large bowl, add pumpkins and use a knife to cut up. Using an immersion blender, mix the pumpkins well. Add seasonings and mix well.

Pour pumpkin into your pot. Add vegetable stock and coconut milk. Hand mix with a large spoon.

Set Instant Pot on High Pressure Manual for 15 minutes. Quick release. Taste your soup. At this time, if you would like to add in more seasonings such as ginger or curry, do as to your own liking. Top soup with croutons and enjoy!

Taco Soup

Ingredients

2 lbs Lean ground beef
1 Low sodium Taco seasoning packet
1 Ranch dressing dry packet
15.25 oz can Southwest corn
(2) 15.25 oz cans Del Monte Zesty Chili diced tomatoes
16 oz can or equivalent Black beans
16 oz can or equivalent Pinto beans
2 oz can Green diced chilies
1 cup Water
Salt and Pepper to taste
Tabasco sauce to taste
1 lb Lean ground beef
1 lb Ground chicken
Olive oil
Avocado

Note:
You can tweak and add in whatever you like to this recipe. Make it your own!

Directions

First, saute your meat in a drizzle of olive oil. I always get my pot warm before I throw in the meat to saute. Using your tempered glass lid, place lid on top and periodically saute meat around with your spatula, being sure all is lightly brown and cooked.

Remove lid and add in your taco seasoning and ranch dressing packets. Mix well and add one cup of water. Stir well. Next, add in the rest of your ingredients, including most all the juices in the can.

Place tempered glass lid back on pot and set your Instant pot to simmer mode. (Simmer mode is actually saute mode in low setting.) Use your adjustment button and plus and minus options to get to the low setting. Simmer for 35 minutes stirring occasionally, and of course having full view of your yummy soup all the while.

Serve topped with avocado, shredded cheese, sour cream, etc. Whatever toppings of your choice. I did simple avocado. Delicious!

Weight Watchers Friendly DEBBIEDOO'S

Tuscan Soup

Ingredients

1 lb Ground turkey

1 Yellow onion, chopped

1 Red bell pepper, chopped

1½ cups Frozen spinach

2 cloves Garlic, chopped

2 cups Low sodium beef broth

1½ tbsp Worcestershire

1 can diced seasoned tomatoes

1 jar of your favorite pasta sauce

2½ cups elbows pasta

Directions

First, saute ground turkey in your pressure cooker on normal setting. Be sure to stir as it sautes. No need to drain fat, as there is very little.

Add onion, pepper, and garlic. Saute on normal for 3 minutes.

Add beef broth, pasta sauces, diced tomatoes, Worcestershire sauce and half cup of water. Set pot on Manual High Pressure for 15 minutes.

Let NPR, then open pot. Add in pasta and spinach. Stir well and set the pot back on for 4 minutes. Always quick release away from cabinets and face!

Enjoy guilt-free!

 This meal has approximately 4 Weight Watchers points per serving!

Weight Watchers Friendly　　DEBBIEDOO'S

Vegetable Soup

Ingredients

1 can diced tomatoes, drained
1 can diced potatoes, drained
1 can French onion soup
1 can Carrots, drained
1 can Green beans, drained
1 can Corn, NOT drained
Maggi seasoning to taste
Salt and Pepper to taste

Note:
All can sizes were
approximately 14.5 oz.

Directions

First, empty soup. Layer one can on top of the other. Pour one cup of water in the pot. DO NOT stir.

Set pot to High Pressure Manual for 5 minutes. Let it naturally release for 1 minute, then slowly quick release. Always be sure your pot is turned away from cabinets and faces!

Enjoy your soup guilt-free!

 This meal has approximately 6 Weight Watchers points per serving!

14

DEBBIEDOO'S

White Bean Chicken Chili

Ingredients

Onions, chopped
2 tbsp Garlic, minced
1 tbsp Olive oil
4 cans (15.5 oz ea) Cannellini beans, rinsed and drained
4 cans (15.5 oz each)
2 cans (14 oz each) Fat-free, reduced-sodium chicken broth
1 can (4.5 oz) Chopped green chile peppers
1 tsp Cumin
1 tsp Salt
¾ tsp Dried oregano
½ tsp. Chili powder
½ tsp Ground black pepper
⅛ tsp Ground red pepper
1½ cups Corn
2.5 lbs Ground chicken
½ cup Chopped green and yellow peppers
1 cup water

Directions

First, saute in olive oil the ground chicken, onion, garlic, salt, pepper, ground red pepper, oregano, chili powder, peppers and cumin all together, mixing well as you are in saute mode.

Once your meat is lightly brown and almost cooked, you can add in your chicken broth, beans, green chilies and corn. Use the manual keys to set the Instant Pot to 13 minutes.

After the cooking has completed, use the quick release lever to release the pressure.

Serve with sliced avocado and parsley for garnishing. Enjoy!

Weight Watchers Friendly   D E B B I E D O O ' S

White Bean Chicken Chili

Ingredients

5-6 Chicken breasts
2 cans Low sodium Northern beans
32 oz Low fat chicken broth
4½ oz can Green chili peppers, chopped
10.2 oz can Low fat Cream of Chicken soup
1 can White hominy
1 packet White bean chili seasoning

Directions

First, cook your chicken breasts in the pressure cooker. I placed the frozen breasts and 1 cup of water in the pot and set to High Pressure Manual for 15 minutes. Let naturally release.

Drain water and shred chicken either with fork or hand mixer right in the pot. Add chili seasoning, soup, broth, 1 can of beans, green chilies and whole can of drained hominy.

Add 1 cup of water. Set the cooker for 5 minutes HP. Quick releas. Add corn starch to thicken and additional can of white beans.

Mix well and serve. Top with shredded Mexican cheese, and green onions. Don't forget the hot sauce on top!

 This meal has approximately 5 Weight Watchers points per serving!

Sides

18 | Corn Pudding Casserole
19 | Deviled Eggs
20 | Homemade Applesauce
21 | Party Meatball Appetizers
22 | Pineapple Puff Casserole
23 | Potato Salad
24 | Stuffing
25 | Weight Watchers Friendly Cauliflower Smashed

Corn Pudding Casserole

Ingredients

½ cup butter, softened

½ cup sugar

1 egg

1 cup (8 oz) sour cream

1 package (8½ oz)
corn bread/muffin mix

½ cup 2% milk

½ can (15¼ oz) whole kernel
corn, drained

½ can (14¾ oz) cream-style
corn

Optional:
Shredded cheddar cheese
for topping

Directions

In a large bowl, add melted butter and sugar until light and fluffy. Add egg, beating well (may hand mix) after each addition.

Beat in sour cream. Gradually add muffin mix alternately with milk. Fold in corn.

Be sure to add foil on the outer ring of your pan. Pour into greased 7" spring form pan.

Set High Pressure Manual 45 to 50 minutes or until set. Quick release and let pudding casserole cool for at least 15 minutes before releasing.

Deviled Eggs

Ingredients

8 Large eggs
2 tbsp Mayonnaise
1 tbsp Extra virgin olive oil
1 tsp Mustard
1 tsp White vinegar
Paprika to taste
Parsley for garnish
Salt and Pepper to taste

Directions

As I mentioned I used the 5-5-5 method in my Instant pot. 5 minutes High manual. 5 minutes Natural release. 5 minutes in an ice bath. One thing I love about these pods is you can place the pod right in the bowl of ice water. So simple just to pick up and plunk in.

For the deviled egg mixture: Slice your eggs length wise right down the center. With a spoon the yolk will simply release out nice and clean. With a fork, smash up the yolks so that there are no large chunks. You want it nice and fluffy. Add the mayonnaise (NOT fat free), mustard, I used a garlic herb yellow base by Heinz.

Add olive oil, vinegar and salt and pepper to taste. I used sea salt. Just a dash will do. Mix well. Spoonful in your empty yolks and top with garnish and paprika. Enjoy!

DEBBIEDOO'S

Homemade Applesauce

Ingredients

10 or more Apples
2 tsp Honey
1 tbsp Cinnamon
2 tsp Ground Cloves
Dash of Salt
1 cup Water
2 Cinnamon Sticks

Directions

Peel and core the apples. In a mixing bowl, combine cinnamon, cloves and salt. Mix well.

Place the cinnamon sticks at the bottom of the Instant Pot. Add your apples and pour one cup of water on top.

Place lid, seal and set to High Pressure Manual for 2 minutes. When it beeps, let it natural release for 1 minute, then do a quick release.

Add honey and mix well with a wooden spoon.

Mash apples with a hand mixer, emergent blender or hand masher. Enjoy yourself or gift to friends!

Party Meatball Appetizers

Ingredients

48 oz Frozen cooked beef
meatballs
18 oz Grape jelly
18 oz Barbecue sauce

Directions

Add 1 cup water to pressure cooking pot. Place a steamer basket in the pressure cooking pot and add frozen meatballs. Pressure cook for 5 minutes on high pressure.

When timer beeps, release the pressure with a QR. Remove steamer basket and meatballs from the pressure cooking pot.

Discard cooking water left in pot and add BBQ sauce and grape jelly to pressure cooking pot. Select Sauté and cook, stirring frequently, until jelly is melted and the sauce is smooth. Add heated meatballs and stir to combine. Just that simple.

Garnish with a little green onion for color and grab your toothpicks! Enjoy!

Pineapple Puff Casserole

Ingredients

6 slices of Bread, cubed
3 Eggs
½ stick Butter
½ cup Sugar
2 tsp Flour
20 oz can Crushed Pineapple

Optional:
1 cup Ham, cubed

Directions

Cube your 6 slices of bread. (With or without crust is fine.) Set pot on saute mode. Add butter and spread evenly. Add cubed bread and toss frequently, browning on both sides.

Remove bread and clean inner pot. Add 1 cup of water to your pot.

In a large bowl, add bread and remaining ingredients. Mix well. If using a spring form pan, be sure to line the outer bottom with foil in case of leakage. Spray pan with non-stick cooking spray. Add your mixture to the pan.

Place pan on a trivet and set in pot. Set to High Pressure Manual for 27 minutes. Quick release when finished and allow to completely cool. Enjoy!

Potato Salad

Ingredients

6 White or Red potatoes
1 cup Water
1 stalk or 2 Celery
1 tbsp Dill
Salt and pepper to taste
¼ cup Red onion
2 spears Dill pickle
4 Hard boiled Eggs
½ cup Mayonnaise
1 tsp Yellow Mustard
1 tsp Cider vinegar

Directions

First, hard boil your eggs according to the method that works for you in your region. I use the 5-5-5 method. You can peel and cut your potatoes first before steaming.

Place potatoes in pressure cooker with water. If you have a steamer basket, great. If not, you can simply add potatoes to the bottom, sitting on top of water. Cook on high pressure for 3 minutes. If potatoes are larger, cook for 4 minutes.

Let steam release for 3 minutes. Then quickly release pressure and open cooker. Peel and dice potatoes when they are cool enough to handle.

Next, layer potatoes, onion, and celery in a large bowl. Season each layer with salt and pepper. Add chopped egg and chopped pickle in between and reserve a few eggs for the top, sliced.

Mix together the mayonnaise, mustard, cider vinegar, and dill pickle in a small bowl. Gently fold the mayonnaise mixture into the potatoes. Chill at least one hour before serving and enjoy!

DEBBIEDOO'S
Stuffing

Ingredients

12 oz cubed bag Herb
seasoned stuffing
1 roll Jimmy Dean's breakfast
sage sausage
2 Red apples, diced
1 cup Celery, diced
1 cup Yellow onion, diced
1 lb Fresh sliced deli Turkey
Turkey gravy
1 cup Chicken broth
(preferably low sodium)
1 cup Water

Directions

Dice apples, celery and yellow onion Turn pot on saute normal mode and add sausage. Lightly season if desired.

Add entire bag of Herb stuffing Add celery, apples and onions on top. Add one cup of chicken broth and one cup of water. Mix well while on normal saute mode to get nice and warm. Shut off Instant pot.

Lightly spray two pans with non-stick butter. Quickly clean out stainless steel inner pot and add one cup of water to the bottom. Add stuffing mixture to the pans. Foil the bottom lip of your pans.

Place one pan on trivet and place in pot. Using the bottom of one of your spring form pans, set that on top of the pan that is on the trivet and gently place the other pan on top. Close lid, seal, and set to High Pressure Manual for 5-7 minutes to heat and combine the flavors.

Carefully quick release and place on a flat platter or plate. After 5-10 minutes, release the spring. Flip the stuffing once completely cool. Top with gravy of choice. Enjoy!

Weight Watchers Friendly   DEBBIEDOO'S

Cauliflower Smashed

Ingredients

1 large head of Cauliflower
½ cup low fat sour cream
Green onions for topping
Garlic to taste
Salt and Pepper to taste
2 tbsp Butter
1 cup Water

Directions

Add a cup of water to pot. Cut up head of cauliflower, removing stem and leaves. Put cauliflower florets into the pot on top of water. You don't need a basket or steamer.

Set pot on High Pressure Manual for 3 minutes. Quick release. Do not drain the water! Let stand for a few minutes before adding next ingredients.

Slowly add in the sour cream, seasoning and butter. Use a hand masher to mash down and mix. Then using an electric mixer, mix on high or medium speed to the consistency you like. If you have an inner stainless steel pot, you can do this all in the pot!

Let stand for a few minutes before serving. Garnish with green onion and enjoy!

 This dish has approximately 3 Weight Watchers points per serving!

Pastas

27   Beef Stroganoff

28   Pesto Pasta Chicken Florentine

29   Ravioli Pie

30   Shrimp Scampi

31   Spaghetti Pie

32   Stuffed Manicotti

33   Vegetable Lasagna

34   Ziti & Sausage in 30 Minutes

DEBBIEDOO'S

Beef Stroganoff

Ingredients

2 lbs stew or pot roast meat,
cubed
1 onion
1 can Campbell's french onion
soup
1 can Golden mushroom soup
2-4 tbsp Worcestershire
(Or more to taste. We love it!)
3-4 cans water
8 oz cream cheese
1 tbsp Garlic salt
1 bag of Yolk egg noodles

Optional:
Baby carrots

Directions

First, saute onions and add your garlic salt and Worcestershire sauce.

I like to brown my meat on both sides first. If using a pot roast cut in parts, I left all the juices as is in the pot and just added the french onion and Golden mushroom soup. Next, add water. Mix well and set pot to High Pressure Manual for 60 minutes.

Cut up the cream cheese into cubes just before serving and add to the pot in low simmer mode. Stir the cream cheese in until it's all combined. (You might have to put the lid back on and leave for 10 minutes.)

You may add corn starch at the end and whisk for a more gravy-like consistency.

Boil noodles as directed on the stove top. Top with sour cream and fresh parsley and enjoy!

Pesto Pasta Chicken Florentine

Ingredients

1 lb Bow tie Pasta

5 Chicken Breasts, cubed

1 cup Sweet yellow onion

1 cup White Wine

5 oz Fresh Spinach

½ cup Heavy cream

½ cup Pesto

3 cloves Minced garlic

Olive oil

Salt and Pepper to taste

Optional:

Pine nuts

Directions

First, cook your pasta. To cook in the pot, use 3 or more cups of water, submerge pasta completely in the water and cook on Manual for 6 minutes with a quick release. Rinse and set aside. (I typically half the time it directs on the pasta box when using the pressure cooker.)

Saute chicken and onion in olive oil until lightly brown. The chicken should be just about cooked. Remove the chicken and onions from the pot. Add minced garlic, heavy cream, wine and pesto. Bring to high heat, stirring consistently.

Add chicken back in the pot and simmer until thoroughly cooked. Add a sprinkle of pine nuts (optional). Remove sauce from pot and set aside.

Add spinach to the pot with a dash of white wine and toss lightly until spinach is simmered down accordingly. Add pasta to your bowl and top with above mixture. If need be, you can add in more wine, pesto and heavy cream to pot to acquire more sauce. Keep in mind, this is a bountiful of flavor and when mixed all together, it is dynamite. Add salt and pepper to taste. Enjoy!

DEBBIEDOO'S
Ravioli Pie

Ingredients

Two variations of tri-colored ravioli
(I use spinach & portabello mushroom)
Approx. 10 frozen meatballs, halved
1 Jar sauce
Italian seasoning to taste
Salt and Pepper to taste
1½ cups shredded mozzarella or Italian blend cheese

Directions

In a 7 inch spring form, layer the bottom of your pan with sauce. Start layering raviolis around the pan, including the center.

Top with meatball, a little sauce and a little shredded cheese.

Continue layering the same until you reach the top. Generously add more cheese, sauce and seasoning.

Add one cup of water to the pot and lower your pan down. Set to High Pressure Manual for 15 minutes. Natural Release for 3 minutes, then Quick Release. Enjoy!

Shrimp Scampi

Ingredients

1 lb Barilla pasta (I used Orcheitta)
16 oz Frozen de-veined cooked shrimp with tail
1 Lemon
5 Cloves crushed garlic
1 cup Chicken broth
½ cup White wine or cooking wine
1 bunch Chopped green scallions
½ stick of Butter
Kosher salt to taste
Pepper to taste
Parsley to taste
Fresh Parmigana cheese

Directions

First, cook your pasta of choice in the Instant Pot. I added 3 cups of water to the pot and a pound of pasta. Set pot on High Pressure for 6 minutes and Quick Release.

Remove pasta, rinse in cold water and set aside. Add 4 tablespoons of butter to pot and set on saute mode.

Once butter is melted, add your chopped garlic and scallions to the pot and continue to stir while on saute until lightly brown.

Add one cup of chicken broth, white wine, a pinch or two of kosher salt, a dash of pepper, and half a squeezed lemon. Continue to stir until a first bubbling of combination. Add in frozen shrimp and stir for a minute or two.

Add in pasta and mix. Add grated cheese, more pepper, and squeeze the other half of lemon in.

Add to serving bowl. Top with parsley, pepper and more cheese to taste.

DEBBIEDOO'S
Spaghetti Pie

Ingredients

1 lb Spaghetti

3 Eggs

Garlic to taste

½ cup grated Parmesan or
Pecorino romano Cheese

½ cup grated Swiss Cheese

½ cupf Mozzarella Cheese

Olive oil

Salt and Pepper to taste

Directions

Partially boil spaghetti in the pot until almost cooked. Strain and rinse noodles with cold water, setting aside.

Lightly grease the bottom and sides of a pan with olive oil. You may wrap the bottom of pan in foil, however there should be no leaking. Set pan aside.

In a large bowl, add spaghetti and drizzle with olive oil until pasta is completely covered and no noodles are sticking together. Lightly salt and pepper. Mix well.

Whisk 3 eggs in a bowl (I added a tad of milk.) Pour eggs over spaghetti and mix well. Add in your cheese blends and again, mix well. Add garlic to taste. Set pot on saute mode. Add two cups of water. Add spaghetti in evenly, patting down with a spatula.

Place pan on a trivet or make a homemade foil sleeve under your pan so you can gently place it in the pot. Cancel out saute option and hit Off. Now start your pot up on Manual High Pressure for 15 minutes.

Natural Release. Remove pie and cool. In about 10-15 minutes, release the Spring-form pan and dive in. This is great served with a crisp side salad. Enjoy!

Stuffed Manicotti

Ingredients

1 box (8 oz) Manicotti shells

16 oz Jar of your favorite sauce

12 oz Ricotta cheese

1 Egg

12 oz Spinach

Shredded Italian blend cheese

Salt and Pepper to taste

Italian seasoning to taste

Directions

In a large bowl, mix 12 oz ricotta and 1 egg. Mix in Italian seasoning, salt and pepper to taste. Add spinach. Mix well. Layer the bottom of your pan with sauce.

Add this ricotta cheese mixture to the shells, being sure to pack it all the way through the entire shell. I used a cheese spreader to push it down and make neat at the end of shells.

Layer your pan with the shells accordingly. I was able to get 4 on the bottom and three on top. In between the first layer, I added more sauce and spread evenly, making sure to get all the shells covered in sauce.Top with shredded cheese and more sauce.

Add one cup of water to the bottom of the pot. Place first pan on a trivet and put a piece of foil on top. Place your other pan on top. Put lid on pot, seal, set to Manual High Pressure for 22 minutes.

Once your pot beeps, do a Quick release. Use silicone mitts to remove pans. (They will be hot, so be careful!) Let cool for 5 minutes and top with remaining warm sauce. Sprinkle more shredded cheese on top and enjoy!

DEBBIEDOO'S

Vegetable Lasagna

Ingredients

1 box Barilla no boil lasagna noodles
1 Jar of your favorite sauce
1 egg
Marzetta roasted red peppers, drained
Salad greens
Spinach
Arugula
20 oz Ricotta cheese
1 bag shredded mozzarella cheese
(I used low fat cheeses)
Italian seasoning to taste
Basil to taste
Garlic to taste
Red pepper flakes to taste
Rosemary to taste
Salt and Pepper to taste

Directions

First, mix ricotta cheese with one egg and seasoning in a bowl. Set aside.

Saute greens in garlic and oil. This only takes a minute or two. Set aside.

Lightly spray 7 inch spring form pan with non-stick spray. Spread an even layer of sauce on the bottom of the pan.

Break noodles, layer to cover bottom of pan. Add a layer of ricotta mixture. Next, add a layer of peppers, greens and mozzarella on top.

Repeat this process to the top of your pan. Top with sauce and mozzarella (1 or 2 bay leaves optional).

Add one cup of water to pot. Set pan on a trivet and set pot to High Pressure for 17 minutes. Quick release.

Let cool before releasing spring form pan. Top with warm sauce and serve!

DEBBIEDOO'S
Ziti & Sausage
in 30 minutes!

Ingredients

4-6 links Italian sweet sausage
½ lb (or a little more) Ziti
1 Jar of your favorite sauce
(My go-to is Victoria brand)
⅓ cup Onions, minced
½ cup Red wine
½ cup Water
Salt and Pepper to taste
Olive oil

Directions

Cut your sausage into bite size pieces.

Lightly drizzle the bottom of you pan with olive oil and saute your sausage and minced onion until lightly brown. (You can find minced dried onion in your grocer spice section.)

Add your favorite jarred sauce. If I am not making fresh sauce, Victoria brand is my go-to. It's really good!

Add your red wine and mix well. Add a dash of salt and pepper to taste. Close lid, be sure it is on seal. Hit Manual setting for 13 minutes.

Quick release. Add pasta, making sure it is submerged in the sauce and wine. Add a half cup of water. Set pot to Manual for 6 minutes

Quick release and mix well. Your dinner is ready!

Beef

36	Apple Beef Stew
37	Cheeseburger Tortilla Pie
38	Cola Pot Roast
39	Corned Beef Brisket
40	Cube Steak
41	Guinness Beef Stew
42	Instant Pot Hamburgers
43	Italian Beef
44	London Broil
45	Instant Pot Meatloaf
46	Philly Cheese Steak Tortilla Pie
47	Rouladen Roll Ups
48	Sirloin Tip Roast
49	Taco Pie

Apple Beef Stew

Ingredients

2 large Fuji Apples
1½ cups Baby carrots
2 cups Apple juice
2 cups Water
2 lbs Beef stew meat
5 whole Cloves
3 whole Allspice
2 Bay leaves
4 tbsp Corn starch
1 whole Yellow onion
½ stick Butter

Directions

Add half a stick of butter to your pot. Set on saute high. Add meat, season well. Add whole onion, mix well.

If you have a tempered glass lid, place on pot and reduce saute to normal setting. Cover your pot and let simmer for at least 20-30 minutes, mixing occasionally in order to reduce any scorching on the bottom. While your meat and onions are sauteing, peel and cube your apples.

After your meat and onions have simmered for the time above, add two cups of apple juice and two cups of water. Mix well.

Add apples, carrots, 5 whole cloves, 3 whole allspice and 4 tablespoons of corn starch and two bay leaves.

Place lid on pot and set to Manual High Pressure for 10 minutes. Do a quick release and add in more cornstarch for a heavier consistency if you desire.

Let stew sit for at least 10 minutes before serving. It is HOT! Enjoy.

DEBBIEDOO'S

DEBBIEDOO'S
Cheeseburger Tortilla Pie

Ingredients

1 lb Ground hamburger
5 Flour tortillas
Hamburger oval dill pickles
Onions
Shredded sharp cheddar
Ranch Dressing
Salt and Pepper to taste
Ketchup
Mustard
Lettuce
Tomato

Directions

First, saute your ground hamburger with onion. Salt and pepper to taste if you wish. You can also add in ketchup and mustard to the saute for flavor. Drain meat and set aside.

Prepare 7 inch pan by lightly spraying the bottom or using parchment paper. Add tortilla shell to bottom and start layering meat, cheese and pickles. Continue until you reach the top of the pan.

Add one cup of water to the pot. Place pan on trivet and lower into pot. Set on High Pressure Manual for 12 minutes.

Natural release for 2 minutes and vent out remaining steam. Let cool for 5 minutes before digging in.

Top with lettuce, tomato and ranch dressing. Enjoy!

DEBBIEDOO'S

Cola Pot Roast

Ingredients

3lbs Chuck roast
4 Carrots, peeled and sliced
1 Onion, sliced
12 oz. can Cola
12. oz. bottle Chili sauce
1 small bag Baby white potatoes
2 tbsp Worcestershire sauce
Salt and Pepper to taste

Directions

My chuck roast was frozen to start, so I added an additional 10 minutes to the pressure time.

First add to your pressure cooker, Cola, Chili sauce, Worcestershire, salt and pepper. Mix well. Add the roast and place onions on top and all around.

Add some pepper to your roast. Close and seal your lid. I chose manual, meat setting for 45 minutes and let natural release.

Add your potatoes and carrots on top of roast. Close lid, seal and hit manual for an additional 8-10 minutes. Then, do a quick release when finished.

Add some fresh thyme if desired. You have a beautiful and tasty roast for your family and friends!

Corned Beef Brisket

Ingredients

2½ - 3 lbs Corned beef brisket
with season packet
4 cups Beef stock
1 Onion, sliced in quarters
4 cloves Garlic
1 small head Cabbage,
cut into quarters
3 large Carrots, cut into thirds
small baby whites Potatoes

Directions

Rinse the corned beef under cold water. Put the seasoning packet, beef broth, onion and garlic into the pressure cooker. Put a rack in the pressure cooker. Place corned beef on rack. Lock the lid in place.

Select High Pressure and set the timer for 75 minutes. When beep sounds, turn off pressure cooker. Use a natural pressure release for 10 minutes, then do a quick pressure release to release any remaining pressure. Carefully remove lid. (Always remember to remove the lid away from your face!)

Remove the rack and brisket from the pressure cooker. Set aside the corned beef and cover in aluminum foil until ready to serve.

Add the potatoes, carrots and cabbage to the broth in the pot. Lock the lid in place and select High Pressure for 4 minutes. If your potatoes at that point still are not quite ready, simply hit saute method for a few more minutes. Dinner is served!

DEBBIEDOO'S
Cube Steak

Ingredients

2 lbs Cube steak (2 packages)
Seasoning for cube steak
(Preferably, Insta-Beef)
1½ cup Water
1 pack Beefy Onion Lipton soup mix
1 tbsp Corn starch

Directions

Season both sides of cube steak. Place cube steak on a trivet (stacked is fine).

Pour 1 cup of water into pot. Lower trivet in pot. Add another half cup of water on top of stacked cubed steak.

Set on High Pressure Manual for 15 minutes. Then, quick release.

While your cube steak is cooking, make your gravy. Mix the pack of beefy onion soup, approx. 1 tablespoon of corn starch, and 1½ cups of water. Whisk while simmering until you get a nice gravy consistency.

Serve a generous amount of gravy on cube steak and mashed potatoes on the side.

DEBBIEDOO'S
Guinness Beef Stew

Ingredients

2 lbs Beef stew meat or chuck
beef roast
2 cups Onion, chopped
1 bag Baby carrots or 3 large
carrots, peeled and cut in chunks
3-4 Parsnips, peeled and chunked
½ lb Yukon potatoes, cut or sliced
6 oz can plain Tomato paste
2 tsp Dried Thyme
4 tbsp Fresh parsley, chopped
1 pint Guinness extra stout
32 oz box Beef broth
Salt and Pepper to taste
½ stick Garlic/Herb butter
1 Shallot
2 cups Green beans

Directions

First, take your half a stick of garlic/herb butter and put in your pot on saute mode. You can use vegetable oil as well, but the butter is so much better.

Place your meat, onions and shallot in the pot and lightly saute, getting everything nice and lightly brown. Add 2 tablespoons of tomato paste. (Only plain tomato paste, nothing with garlic, or basil, etc.) Stir well.

Add your bottle of Guinness and beef broth. Hit the stew/meat option button on your pressure cooker and set for 30 minutes on normal pressure.

Once the cycle is finished, you can do a quick release and then add in all your vegetables, carrots, potatoes, green beans and remaining tomato paste. Stir well. Be sure to submerge all the vegetables in the broth.

Close lid, seal and set on manual for 6-7 minutes. Quick release when finished. Serve with a side of sour dough bread and enjoy!

Instant Pot Hamburgers

Ingredients

2 lbs Ground beef
(Sirloin or chuck hamburger meat)
1 Egg
1 cup Bread crumbs
1 Red onion, chopped
Tabasco sauce
Worcestershire sauce
Cheddar cheese
Salt and Pepper to taste
Beef rub seasoning

Directions

In a mixing bowl, combine your meat, egg, bread crumbs, Tabasco to taste, Worcestershire sauce to taste, and one chopped red onion.

Form hamburger patties and make a thumb print in the middle of the patty.

Wrap each individually with aluminum foil and add beef seasoning on top. Stack burgers on a trivet.

Add one cup of water to the pot and lower trivet. Set on High Pressure Manual for 12 minutes. Let cool for one minute before placing on bun. Enjoy!

Italian Beef

Ingredients

3 lbs Sirloin tip roast
16 oz jar Giardiniera
Chopped Roasted garlic
Yellow onion
Salt and Pepper to taste
Vegetable oil
2 cups Beef Broth
Thyme to taste

Optional:

Italian Dressing Packet

Directions

Drain most of the juice from the Giardiniera jar. (My husband had everything marinating for about 30 minutes before he added it to the pot.)

Add a drizzle of vegetable oil on the bottom of your inner pot. Saute sirloin first. Lightly season with salt and pepper and saute your meat on both sides.

Add remainder of the mixture into the pressure cooker. Close lid, turn to seal and set on Manual High Pressure for 45 minutes. Let natural release.

Serve on an Italian crusty roll with the side of your choice! Be sure to add the au jus on the roll and even have a little bowl on the side for dipping. Delish!

DEBBIEDOO'S
London Broil

Ingredients

2 lbs London Broil

1 can Stout Beer
(or any dark beer will suffice)

1 bottle BBQ sauce

1 tsp Brown sugar

¼ cup Onion flakes

Salt and Pepper to taste

Directions

First, add the BBQ sauce, 1 can of beer, brown sugar, salt, pepper and onion flakes to the pot. Mix all ingredients well.

Cut the London Broil in half and place it in the pot. Set to manual/meat option High Pressure for 35 minutes.

Natural release when finished and BAM... That's it! Dynamite dinner!

Instant Pot Meatloaf

Ingredients

2 lbs Ground sirloin
¼ cup Chili sauce
1 Dry Onion soup packet
¼ cup Worcestershire
1 cup Italian style bread crumbs
Salt and Pepper to taste
½ cup Water
2 tbsp Milk

Optional:
2 Eggs, hard-boiled

Directions

Set your pot to saute and add a cup of water to the bottom. In a separate bowl, mix all ingredients, being sure your mixture is combined well. Lightly spray the bottom of your Bundt pan or regular spring form pan with cooking spray. Add your first layer of meatloaf to the pan, spreading it around evenly. Use your clean hands or spatula to pat down as you go.

Optional: Add in hard boiled eggs for a bit of interest. Form two gullies and add your whole hard boiled eggs in each gully.

Add the remaining meatloaf on top, covering the eggs if you added them. Pat down evenly and smooth out the loaf. Top with chili sauce, salt and pepper or seasoning of your choice.

Wrap the bottom of your spring form pan tightly with foil. There is no doubt you will get some slight leaking from the fat and juices from the loaf. Set your pot on Manual High Pressure for 38 minutes. (Always be sure to put a cup of water in the pot.)

Quick release. Remove the pan gently and rest on a wire wrack or plate to cool. Remove the spring form pan. Place a plate over the loaf and flip gently. Serve with mashed potatoes home fries and a vegetable of choice. Enjoy!

DEBBIEDOO'S
Philly Cheese Steak Tortilla Pie

Ingredients

2 Green bell Peppers
1 large Yellow onion
2 lbs Angus beef steak
(1 lb per pie)
10 Soft tortilla shells
(5 tortillas per pie)
Provolone cheese
(1 slice per layer)
Salt and Pepper to taste
Au Jus Gravy packet

Note:

Makes two pies.

Directions

First, slice green peppers, onions and steak. Set pot to saute mode, add olive oil and let heat. Throw in the pepper and onions. Saute until golden and soft. Remove from pot and set aside.

Repeat the same process, adding beef and seasoning with salt and pepper. When meat is brown on both sides, add in Au Jus and one cup of water. Stir and set pot to High Pressure Manual for 12 minutes.

Quick release. Remove steak and gravy from pot. Add gravy to a gravy boat and set aside for later topping.

Prepare two 7 inch pans with light olive oil spray. Add tortilla and start layering with steak, peppers and a slice of provolone. Repeat to the top of the pan. (Should take 5 layers each pan.)

Add one cup of water to Instant Pot. Set pan on a trivet and lower into pot. Set to High Pressure Manual for 15 minutes. If making two at a time, they will work in the 8 qt. stacked and foiled on top. Enjoy topped with Au Jus!

Rouladen Roll Ups

Ingredients

Flank Steak
(1 package made 10 rolls)
1 Onion
3 Dill pickles
Diced prosciutto or bacon
1 Beef steak tomato
1 packet Beef bourguignon
1⅓ cups Red wine
1½ cups Water
Mustard to taste
4 tbsp Butter

Directions

Dice your onion and pickle. Add 2 tablespoons of butter to Instant Pot and set on saute. Add onion, pickle and proscuitto to the pot and stir repeatedly until lightly golden and soft. Remove from pot and be sure to scrape bits off the bottom.

Tenderize your flank steak accordingly. Slice in strips approximately 5 inches wide.

Spread a thin layer of mustard (spicy or regular) over meat. Add your onion, pickle and proscuitto on top, spreading evenly. Gently roll and tie.

Add another few tablespoons of butter to the pot and set on saute. Lightly brown both sides of rolled beef.

Mix your sauce with wine, one cup of water, and add in diced tomato. Pour over beef and set pot on High Pressure Manual for 20 minutes.

Let natural release for 5 minutes. Serve with a hearty egg noodle. Enjoy!

Sirloin Tip Roast

Ingredients

3-4 lbs Sirloin Tip Roast
1 packet Maggi Pot Roast
seasoning mix
Garlic Cloves
Red Onion
Pepper

Directions

First, cut 3 slits on top of roast and stuff with garlic cloves. (Half a clove is fine.)

Heavily season roast on both sides with pepper. Place roast on a trivet rack.

Mix seasoning packet with water accordingly and pour over roast. Add red onion slices on top.

Set your pot to High Pressure Manual for 50 minutes. Add an additional cup of water to the pot. Do not pour water over the meat, pour it on the side into the pot.

Note: If you want to go more on the pink side, try cutting the time perhaps by 10 minutes off this recipe. The internal temp should be between 135-145.

Let pot naturally release. Remove roast and pour sauce generously on top. Cut accordingly to serve with a side of your choice. Dinner is served!

DEBBIEDOO'S
Taco Pie

Ingredients

1 lb Ground Beef, 95% lean

16 oz can Refried beans

16 oz Diced tomatoes with
green chilies

1 package Shredded
Mexican cheese

1 packet Taco seasoning
(low sodium)

1⅓ cup Water

5-6 round Flour tortillas

Optional Toppings:

Shredded Lettuce

Salsa

Guacamole

Directions

Saute ground beef. Drain the meat accordingly. Add taco seasoning packet along with 1/3 cup water and just a few spoonfuls of diced tomatoes.

Prep pan while meat sautes. Add a foil lip under spring form pan in case of leakage. Remove meat from inner pot. Clean pot and set back in your pressure cooker.

Lightly spray 7 inch spring form pan with cooking spray. Layer one flour tortilla on the bottom. Next, take your refried beans and lightly layer on top. Add a layer of ground beef, then a layer of diced tomatoes. Sprinkle cheese on top. Repeat the same process until you get to the top of pan. (Should be 5 layers.) I topped mine with the diced tomatoes, cheese and added a few spicy chipotle peppers.

Place pan on trivet or homemade foil sleeve to lower pan into pressure cooker. Add a cup of water to pot and set to High Pressure Manual for 15 minutes.

Quick release. Remove pan to cool for at least 10 minutes. Slice and serve, adding more tomatoes or topping of choice. Enjoy!

Pork

51 | Apple Bourbon Pork Tenderloin
52 | Cream Soda Ribs
53 | Pork Fried Rice
54 | Pork Loin Stuffed Roast

Apple Bourbon Pork Tenderloin

Ingredients

2 seasoned Apple bourbon
pork tenderloins (or any
seasoned loin of choice)
1 cup Apple juice
Red cabbage in a jar
1 Apple, sliced
1 can beer ½ full
(I used a lager)

Directions

Wrap two pork tenderloins around the Insta-Rack, one on each side, to make a perfect circle.

Add potatoes on skewers of rack, washed and lightly salted. Add beer can to center of rack.

Add one cup of apple juice to the pressure cooker.

Lower rack into the pot. Pour red cabbage on top of loin and can. Add sliced apple.

Set pot to High Pressure Manual for 18 minutes. Quick release.

Using mitts, carefully remove the rack and set on a plate to cool. Serve as is on table and help yourself!

Cream Soda Ribs

Ingredients

3.13 used or more St. Louis
Pork Ribs
1 can Cream soda
(or soda of choice)
Rub seasoning
Salt and Pepper to taste
Olive oil

Directions

Remove the membrane from the back of your ribs. Use a butter knife to slip under and peel it back. Blot your rack of ribs with a paper towel.

Drizzle olive oil on the ribs along with salt and pepper. Generously add your rub seasoning to both front and back of ribs. Gently knead the meat with the rub to be sure it will penetrate. Lightly drizzle soda.

Add a cup of water to your pot, along with a dash of the soda. Gently wrap ribs around rack and place the soda can in the center. You can also wrap ribs around the inner pot just the same and add can of soda to the pot. Set your pot to manual High Pressure for 24 minutes or to your own liking of tenderness. Between 16-30 minutes is the level of tenderness you will achieve.

Once finished, do a Quick release and remove ribs. You can then place them on a foil lined cookie sheet or pan and put on broil for 10 minutes. I did also add a little more soda on top before I broiled, and then after I broiled. So good! Serve with a fresh salad and beans. Enjoy!

Pork Fried Rice

Ingredients

3 tbsp Canola oil

1 sliced and diced Yellow onion

12 oz Baby rainbow colored carrots

2 lbs Boneless thin pork chops, cubed

1 Egg

Salt and Pepper to taste

2 cups Uncle Ben's rice

1½ cups Chicken broth

1½ cups Water

Directions

Select saute. Once your pot is hot, add onions and carrots. Continue to saute until onion is lightly brown.

Add your beaten egg and cubed pork. Saute, continually stirring until lightly brown. Remove mixture of onion, pork and carrots. Scrape bits if needed but leave them in the pot. Add 1½ cups of chicken broth. Add 1½ cups of water. Add 2 cups of Uncle Ben's long grain white or brown rice. (Not instant rice.)

Return the pork, carrots and onion to the pot. Be sure everything is submerged and covered in liquid. Place lid on pot and hit rice option. Set time for 12 minutes.

Let naturally release for 10 minutes. Stir well before serving. Add soy sauce on top if desired. (We actually used Maggi.) Enjoy your perfect pork fried rice!

Pork Loin Stuffed Roast

Ingredients

5-6 lbs Pork Loin

1½ cups pears, diced

1 cup Canned Cranberries

1 cup Walnuts, chopped

½ stick Butter

½ cup Brown sugar

Pear juice from one can of pears

Directions

Turn your pressure cooker on saute mode high and add half a stick of butter. Once heated, add pears, cranberries and walnuts. Cover with tempered glad lid and let simmer for about 10 minutes, mixing in between.

Add brown sugar and pear juice. Simmer for 5 minutes. Remove all above ingredients to another bowl and set aside. Rinse out inner pot of pressure cooker and add 1 cup of water to the pot.

Place your pork loin on a large piece of tin foil. Butterfly your pork loin. Lightly season inside and add a layer of your mixture from the bowl. Fold loin and add either cooking tie or toothpicks to keep closed.

Loosely enclose the loin with the foil and place loin on a trivet. Put in the pot. Set to Manual High Pressure for 50 minutes. Once it beeps, do a quick release. Remove roast and drizzle more of your combination of pears, cranberries and walnuts on top. Place your loin under the broiler for 5-7 minutes. You may again add more juices on top. Cool, cut and enjoy!

Chicken

56 | Beer Can Chicken
57 | Bruschetta Chicken
58 | Buffalo Chicken Tortilla Pie
59 | Chicken Cacciatore
60 | Chicken Curry
61 | Chili Cranberry Chicken
62 | Cream of Chicken
63 | Fajita Pie
64 | Tuscan Chicken (with Spinach & Pine Nuts)
65 | Weight Watchers Friendly Chicken Teriyaki
66 | Weight Watchers Friendly Shredded Spicy Mango Chicken
67 | Weight Watchers Friendly Sweet & Sour Chicken

Beer Can Chicken

Ingredients

4-5 lbs Chicken
Olive oil, brushed on bird
Rub or Seasoning of choice
1 Lemon
One can beer or soda of choice
(room temperature preferably)
1 cup Broth (chicken or
vegetable)

Note:
You can spill a little of the beer
or soda into the pot as well.

Directions

Clean chicken and remove gizzards. Pat dry and brush on olive oil. Generously rub chicken with your choice of rub or seasoning. Be sure to penetrate the flavors.

Place beer can in the center of the rack. Gently sit bird on top of can through the open cavity. Push it down as far as you can and bring the chicken legs out in a sitting position.

Add your broth to the bottom of the pot and squeeze some lemon inside. Add half the lemon to the pot. Lift your rack and set gently down in pot. Maneuver, tuck or tilt chicken to place the lid on. Be sure to seal.

Set pot to Manual High Pressure for 13-15 minutes. Because times vary and the chicken cooks fast, I recommend starting off with less time and adding more as needed. Quick release. Allow an additional 15 minutes for the pot to come to pressure.

If to the proper temperature, (safe internal temp is 165° F) gently lift rack out and broil for 5-7 minutes for a nice crisp. (Use a drip pan under chicken.) Before serving, squeeze on the other half of lemon and enjoy!

DEBBIEDOO'S

Bruschetta Chicken

Ingredients

4-6 pieces Chicken cutlets
or Chicken breasts
Slices Mozzarella cheese
Fresh Basil
Minced garlic
Olive oil
Balsamic glaze
1 can Basil/Garlic/Oregano
flavored Diced Tomatoes
Italian style bread crumbs
Salt and Pepper to taste

Note:
Add ingredients to your own taste and liking. Some like it heavy on the garlic, while others just like a hint of garlic.

Directions

Drizzle your inner pot with olive oil. Next, add minced garlic to taste. I added around 3 teaspoons.

Trim chicken fat. If you can't find thin Chicken cutlets at your local grocery, simply butterfly your chicken breasts in half. Lightly sprinkle chicken breasts with Italian style bread crumbs, salt, pepper and fresh basil.

On saute mode normal setting, lightly brown chicken breasts on both sides. Add can of diced tomatoes and cook in manual for 9 minutes. Do a quick release.

On a baking sheet lined with foil, add your chicken breast and diced tomato topping, being sure all the breasts are covered in tomatoes and juice. Top each breast with a slice of mozzarella cheese.

Broil until the cheese is melted, light brown and bubbly. Remove chicken and place on a platter. Drizzle a Balsamic glaze and add more fresh basil on top. Looks so nice and ohhh so fancy...Yum! Enjoy with a side, pasta, or salad.

DEBBIEDOO'S

Buffalo Chicken Tortilla Pie

Ingredients

1 to 1.5 lb Chicken Breast
5 soft Tortillas
(for tacos and fajitas)
1 cup Ken's Buffalo Wing
sauce
Blue Cheese Dressing
Celery seed or salt
Celery
Carrots

Directions

Add a cup of water to pot. Cook chicken breasts on High Pressure for 15 minutes, then natural release. Remove chicken and drain water. Rinse pot.

In a separate bowl, add one cup of Buffalo wing sauce on top of chicken breasts. Using a fork or hand mixer, shred chicken. (Chicken should be tender.) Lightly spray your 7 inch pan with non-stick spray. Foil the outer bottom of pan in case of leakage.

Layer bottom of pan with tortilla, then chicken, a dash of celery seed or salt, and a dollop of blue cheese dressing. Repeat layering to the top of the pan. On the top tortilla, you may add a little more wing sauce and celery seed or salt.

Add one cup of water to your pot. Set pan on a trivet. Set pot on High Pressure Manual for 15 minutes. Quick release and let cool for 5 minutes before serving. Serve with a side of celery, carrots and blue cheese.

You may also top pie with shredded lettuce, carrots and blue cheese. Enjoy!

DEBBIEDOO'S
Chicken Cacciatore

Ingredients

28 oz can Crushed tomatoes
15 oz can Seasoned diced
tomatoes
10 Chicken drumsticks
Peppers (red, yellow, green)
Onion
(I use a frozen bag of Birds Eye)
1-2 cloves Garlic
3 Bay leaves
Basil to taste
Salt and Pepper to taste
dash of Red Wine

Directions

Saute chicken drumsticks in a little bit of olive oil on normal setting. (Be sure to let oil warm up before adding drumsticks.) Add sliced garlic, season chicken with basil, salt and pepper. Brown on each side. Remove chicken and set aside.

Add crushed tomatoes, diced tomatoes, splash of red wine and a little more seasoning to taste. Add chicken back in and submerge in sauce.

Add one cup of water and set on High Pressure for 15 minutes. Let natural release.

Open pot and add in peppers. If frozen, simply set to saute for 5 minutes to warm. If fresh, close pot and cook for an additional 15 minutes.

Dinner is served!

Chicken Curry

Ingredients

2-3 lbs skinless, boneless
Chicken breast
1 can Coconut milk
2 tbsp Curry powder
1 tbsp Turmeric
1 tbsp Cumin
½ Onion, thinly sliced
14.5 oz can Diced tomatoes
½ cup Greek yogurt
½ cup Water
3 Yukon gold potatoes, diced

Topping:
Cilanro
Lemon juice

Directions

Set Instant Pot on saute mode. Add a little vegetable oil to the bottom of the pot. Add onions and saute until caramelized. Scrape off bits that may be sticking to the bottom.

Place chicken in pot and add your can of tomatoes on top.

In a mixing bowl, add coconut milk, turmeric, cumin, curry powder, water and yogurt. Whisk and mix well.

Pour mixture over chicken and tomatoes. Set pot to meat or Manual High Pressure for 35 minutes.

Let natural release. Remove chicken, then put your diced potatoes in the pot for approximately 7-8 minutes. Quick release.

Add all in a serving bowl and top with cilantro and a squeeze of lemon juice. Basmanti or Jasmine rice is the perfect compliment to this meal!

DEBBIEDOO'S
Chili Cranberry Chicken

Ingredients

1 cup Chili sauce

1 cup Whole berry cranberry sauce

3 tbsp Orange marmalade

⅛ tsp Ground allspice

6 skinless Chicken breasts

Directions

Set your pot on saute mode. Add 3 teaspoons of vegetable oil to the pot and let warm. Saute chicken on both sides. Remove from pot.

Combine all ingredients and pour over chicken breasts. Using a pan inside the pot is optional.

Add one cup of water to the pot and set on High Pressure Manual for 12 minutes. Let naturally release and serve over rice. Enjoy!

Cream of Chicken

Ingredients

10 oz can low fat
Cream of Chicken soup
10-12 oz can Roasted corn
1 cup French's red bell pepper
crunchy onion toppers
Paprika to taste
Salt and Pepper to taste
2 tsp Butter
5-6 Chicken breasts

Directions

Turn pot on saute mode and add butter. Cut your chicken breasts in half. Add chicken to pot and season with salt and pepper to taste. Saute on both sides to golden. Remove chicken and clean pot.

In a separate bowl, mix soup, corn and paprika to your liking. (I added 1 tablespoon.) Add half a cup of French's onion toppers. Mix well.

Foil the bottom of your pan. Layer pan with mixture. Add chicken on top. Add remaining mixture on top of chicken.

Add one cup of water to the pot. Place pan on a trivet or homemade foil sling for easy in and out of pot. Set pot to High Pressure Manual for 15 minutes.

Let pot naturally release. Remove pan and let cool. Add remaining French's onion topping. Serve with a side of rice and enjoy!

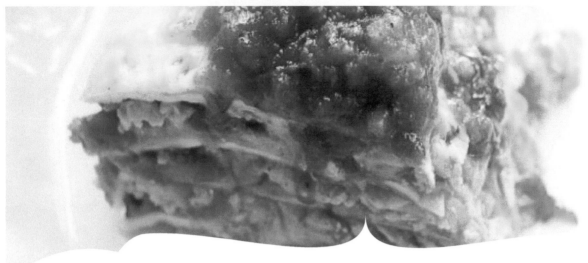

DEBBIEDOO'S

Fajita Pie

Ingredients

1 lb Ground chicken

15.5 oz can Refried beans

12 oz Peppers (red, orange, yellow) and Onion (frozen or freshly chopped)

1 liquid packet Fajita sauce, seasoned and ready for use

1 bag Mexican cheese

Salsa to taste

Flour or wheat tortillas

Directions

Lightly drizzle bottom of your inner pot with olive oil. Saute the ground chicken, adding in just a little fajita sauce. Remove ground chicken and set aside.

Add more olive oil as needed to saute peppers and onions. Saute on high until lightly brown. Remove from pot and set aside.

Turn on pot to saute and start heating up. Foil the bottom of your pan to catch any excess liquids. Start with one layer of tortilla on the bottom of your lightly sprayed pan. Spread a thin layer of refried beans, then peppers and onions, spreading evenly. Add chicken evenly on top and lightly add fajita sauce and salsa. Top with cheese. Next, grab another flour tortilla and repeat the same layers, being sure to flatten your tortillas in between.

Place your pan on a trivet. If you do not have one, make a homemade one using foil to create a sling to easily lower your pan down. Add a cup of water to the pot. Set your pot to 15-17 minutes on High Pressure Manual.

Once time is up, do a Quick release. Remove pan and let cool for at least 5 minutes before releasing the sling. Slice and serve with your favorite toppings. Lettuce, sour cream, olives, etc!

Tuscan Chicken

Ingredients

2.5 lbs Chicken Breast

2 cups Tuscany chicken broth
(Progresso or any broth on hand)

2 oz Pine nuts

2 tbsp Garlic

2 cups Plum tomatoes

½ cup Sun dried tomatoes

Lemon to taste

16 oz Spinach

Olive oil

Salt and Pepper to taste

Tortellini according to servings

Optional:

Artichoke hearts

Directions

Set pot to normal saute mode. Drizzle bottom of pot with olive oil. Saute pine nuts to a golden brown. Remove from pot.

Add chicken breasts and garlic to pot. Lightly brown on both sides. Add in broth. On top of chicken, add pine nuts, tomatoes, sun dried tomatoes, lemon to taste and optional artichoke hearts. Do not mix.

Set pot on Manual High Pressure for 15 minutes. Let pot natural release.

Open pot and add the spinach. Lightly mix until the spinach is tender.

Serve this dish over tortellini or pasta of choice. May add fresh grated cheese and parsley. Enjoy!

Weight Watchers Friendly   DEBBIEDOO'S
Chicken Teriyaki

Ingredients

2½ lbs Chicken breast,
skinless and cubed
½ cup of Honey
½ cup of Soy Sauce
1 tbsp on Hot chili sauce
1 tbsp of Sweet chili sauce
1 tbsp Worcestershire
3 whole Garlic cloves
1 cup of Water

Directions

Add chicken to the Instant Pot. Pour all ingredients on top of chicken. Do not mix.

Set pot on High Pressure Manual for 14 minutes. When time is up, do a quick release and serve over rice. That's it!

I also recommend scallions on top for additional flavor. Enjoy!

 This meal has approximately 8 Weight Watchers points per serving! (Including one cup of rice!)

Weight Watchers Friendly DEBBIEDOO'S
Shredded Spicy Mango Chicken

Ingredients

4 Chicken breasts
14 oz Mango chunky salsa
(You can add fresh diced mango to a traditional salsa)
1 Fresh mango
Jamaican hot sauce
Salt to taste

Directions

Add 1 cup of water to your pot. Lightly salt chicken breasts. Place chicken breasts on a trivet or steamer rack. Pour half the salsa on top of chicken.

Set pot on High Pressure Manual for 15 mintues. Let it come to natural release (takes about 10 minutes).

Remove chicken and drain water from the pot. You should still have some salsa on top of the chicken.

Add chicken back into the pot and pour remaining salsa on top. Add hot sauce to your liking. Shred chicken with a hand mixer. Dice mango to add on top of shredded chicken. Mix well and serve with rice, on rolls, or just plain with a side salad!

 This meal has approximately 4 Weight Watchers points per serving! (Not including roll.)

Weight Watchers Friendly   DEBBIEDOO'S

Sweet & Sour Chicken

Ingredients

4 Chicken breasts, trimmed and cubed

Onion flakes (just a dash)

¼ tsp Garlic powder

12 oz Sweet and sour sauce

8 oz Chunked pineapple with juice

1 head of Broccoli (cut in heads)

Tri-colored peppers and onions (frozen)

1 cup Water

Butter or Vegetable oil

Optional:

1 tbsp Brown Sugar

Directions

Set your pot to saute mode. Add a little vegetable oil or butter to the pot. Let warm first.

Add cubed chicken and seasoning. Lightly brown chicken on both sides. Add sweet and sour sauce and one cup of water.

Set pot to High Pressure Manual for 10 mintues. Let natural release for 3 minutes, then do a quick release.

Add in broccoli, pineapple and peppers. Set for 2 minutes High Pressure. Quick Release when finished and serve over rice. Enjoy guilt free!

 This meal has approximately 7 Weight Watchers points per serving!

Holiday Treats

69	Christmas Wreath Cake
70	Gingerbread Pumpkin Cake
71	Patriotic Flower Cake
72	Spring Flower Cake
73	Sugar Cookie Fudge

Christmas Wreath Cake

Ingredients

1 Duncan Hines cake mix
(I used French Vanilla)
12 oz flavored Seltzer
(Cranberry-lime)

Optional Toppings:
Frosting
Strawberries, sliced
Blueberries
Blackberries
Fresh mint

Directions

In a bowl, mix the cake mix and flavored seltzer soda by hand. Do not add in anything extra.

Lightly spray pan with non-stick baking spray and add your mixture.

Add one cup of water to the Instant Pot. Set pot to High Pressure Manual for 35 minutes. Quick release and let cake cool 10 to 15 minutes before releasing spring form.

Flip the cake over. Frost if you wish and decorate with fruit, strawberries, blueberries, fresh mint, etc. Use a cute ornament to top your cake if you wish! Enjoy your holiday!

Gingerbread Pumpkin Cake

Ingredients

1 Yellow cake mix

3 eggs

1 cup Pumpkin pie filling

1 tsp Allspice

1 tsp Ground nutmeg

1 tbsp Ground ginger

½ cup Vegetable oil

Directions

Mix the boxed cake according to directions, *minus* the water. Add the pumpkin pie filling. Mix well for at least two to three minutes. (I used a whisk in lieu of a hand mixer.) Add spices and mix well again.

Prep your bundt pan with cooking spray. Pour in batter.

Add one cup of water to the Instant Pot. Set on High Pressure Manual for 40 minutes. Some times may vary.

Note: If you have sections of the cake where the pumpkin pie filling is not cooked, don't fret! It's like a delicious filling and your cake is most certainly cooked through with the eggs in it!

Quick release and let cool in pan for at least 30 minutes before releasing the spring form. Once cool, flip cake over. You can decorate by sprinkling ginger snaps or drizzling icing as pictured.

Top with a scoop of vanilla ice cream and enjoy!

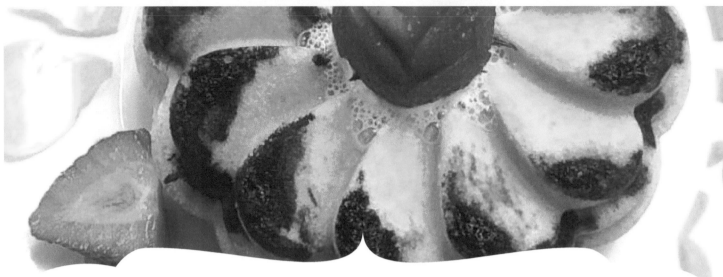

DEBBIEDOO'S

Patriotic Flower Cake

Ingredients

1 Yellow or White box
cake mix
Cool whip
Strawberries
Blue food coloring

Directions

In a mixing bowl, make the cake batter according to instructions on the box. Typically 3 eggs, 1 cup of water and 1/3 cup of vegetable oil.

Prepare flower pan by lightly spraying the bottom with non-stick butter spray. Add a few droplets of food coloring to the pan and swirl around. You can swirl also getting the ribs of the second and third flower layer.

Add half the mixed batter to the pan, being sure it is layered evenly all around.

Add 1 cup of water to your pot. Use trivet or a homemade foil sling to easily lower the pan into the pot. Set pressure cooker to High Pressure Manual for 23-25 minutes.

Quick release when finished. Remove cake and let stand 7 minutes before flipping over onto a plate.

Decorate accordingly for the season or holiday. Enjoy!

DEBBIEDOO'S

Spring Flower Cake

Ingredients

1 box White cake mix
(Duncan Hines preferably)
2 cups Coconut
Food coloring of choice
(I used green)
Jell-O packet flavor of choice
(I used orange)
Fruit of choice
(I used mandarin oranges)
Cool Whip topping

Directions

In a bowl, empty contents of White cake mix and Jell-O. Mix box cake according to directions. Mix well.

Prepare 7 inch spring form or bundt pan with non-stick cooking spray. Add mixed cake to the pan and spread evenly.

Add one cup of water to the pot. Place pan on a trivet. Lower down into the pressure cooker and set to High Pressure Manual for 45 minutes. Quick release. Remove cake and set to cool.

Once cool, remove cake from pan and place on a plate. Frost cake with Cool Whip.

In a separate bowl, mix coconut with food coloring of choice. I used about 10 drops to get my desired color. Sprinkle this on top of the cake.

Add fruit of choice to the center of the cake. Only cut cake a little past halfway to form your flower. Enjoy this spring treat!

Sugar Cookie Fudge

Ingredients

2 bags 12 oz each white
chocolate chip morsels
1¼ cup pre-packaged Sugar
cookie mix
14 oz can Condensed
sweetened milk

Optional:
Festive sprinkles!

Directions

Add two cups of water to the Instant Pot. Next, place a Pyrex glass dish on top that fits the opening of the pot. It should be able to rest on top.

Melt chocolate in the dish. This takes about 10 minutes to completely melt.

Note: Be careful when melting the chocolate to hold onto the Pyrex dish with an oven mitt as you stir.

Once melted, set the pot on warm. In a separate bowl, add sugar cookie mix and condensed sweetened milk. Mix well. Add melted chocolate and mix completely well again.

Line an 8x8 pan with parchment paper. Pour fudge mixture into the pan and spread evenly. Top with sprinkles.

Let cool in the refrigerator for two hours before cutting. Enjoy!

Desserts

75	Apple Crisp Delight
76	Applesauce Walnut Raisin Cake
77	Blueberry Cheesecake
78	Coca-Cola Cake
79	Cranberry Orange & Thyme Monkey Bread
80	Crownie
81	Lemon Supreme Cake
82	Peanut Clusters
83	Pineapple Cream Cheese Upside Down Cake
84	Pumpkin Bread Pudding
85	Pumpkin Cheesecake
86	Spiced Pear & Cranberry Cake
87	Weight Watchers Friendly Upside Down Apple Pie
88	Weight Watchers Friendly Pumpkin Banana Cake

Apple Crisp Delight

Ingredients

5 apples
½ cup water
½ tsp nutmeg
2 tsp cinnamon
4 tbsp butter
¼ cup flour
¾ rolled oats
¼ cup brown sugar
½ teaspoon salt
1 tsp maple syrup

Directions

Peel your apples and cut into bite size chunks. Place on the bottom of your pressure cooker. Sprinkle apples with cinnamon, nutmeg and maple syrup.

Please make sure to spray lightly the bottom of pot with non-stick cooking spray. Pour water over mixture. In a separate bowl, melt your butter. Mix oats, butter, flour, brown sugar and salt. Drop your mixture on top of the apples, water and syrup that are in the pressure cooker. Being sure to cover mixture evenly.

Secure the lid, turn the seal. Hit manual for 8 minutes, high pressure. Let your pot NP (Natural release). Let combination sit for a few minutes. Serve immediately. Don't forget a scoop of vanilla ice cream to go with!

Applesauce Walnut Raisin Cake

Ingredients

1 Cake mix of choice
(yellow, white or spice)
1½ cups Cinnamon applesauce
1 cup Golden Raisins

Optional:
½ cup Walnuts, chopped
1 Egg

Directions

In a bowl, combine your cake, applesauce, raisins and walnuts. Mix well.

Do not add in oil or water. You may add 1 egg if you desire, but then do not add in the other ½ cup of applesauce.

Add mix to a 7 inch bundt pan or cake pan. Lower pan into pot using a trivet or homemade foil sleeve.

Note: Don't forget to foil wrap the outer bottom of the pan just in case there is any small leakage.

Add 1 cup of water to your pot. Set pressure cooker to High Pressure Manual for 30 minutes. Quick release when finished and remove cake to cool. Enjoy this tasty treat!

DEBBIEDOO'S

Blueberry Cheesecake

Ingredients

16 oz Cream cheese
1 cup Sour cream
1½ tsp Vanilla extract
2 Eggs
1 cup Sugar
1 tbsp Corn starch
½ cup Melted butter
2 cups Keebler graham
cracker crumbs
21 oz Blueberry pie filling

Directions

Grease a 7 inch spring form pan. In a medium mixing bowl, combine graham cracker crumbs and melted butter. Place crumb and butter mixture into spring form pan and pat down evenly until firm. Put the pan in the freezer.

In a large mixing bowl, beat cream cheese on medium speed until fluffly. Add sugar, cornstarch and vanilla extract. Beat until combined.

Add eggs, one at a time, beating until just combined after each one. Stir in sour cream. Evenly pour this mixture into the spring form pan.

Add 1½ cups water to the bottom of inner pot. Place cheesecake pan on a trivet above the water. Set on Manual for 25 minutes, then natural release.

Remove cheesecake and trivet. Lightly blot excess moisture from the top of the cake with a paper towel. Top with blueberry pie filling and refrigerate cheesecake for 4 hours. Enjoy!

DEBBIEDOO'S

Coca-Cola Cake

Ingredients

1 Boxed chocolate cake mix
(Duncan Hines preferably)
10 oz Coke (Diet or regular)

Optional:
½ cup chocolate chips
Walnuts

Directions

In a bowl, empty contents of chocolate cake mix. Add soda and other optional mentioned ingredients. (Do not be tempted to add eggs and oil to the mix!) Mix well.

Prepare 7 inch spring form pan with non-stick cooking spray. Add mixed cake to the pan and spread evenly.

Add one cup of water to the pot. Place pan on a trivet and lower down into the pressure cooker.

Set to High Pressure Manual for 35 minutes. Then, quick release. That's it!

Remove cake and set to cool. Serve with whipped cream or ice cream! Enjoy!

Cranberry Orange & Thyme Monkey Bread

Ingredients

2 cans Southern style biscuits
1 Orange
½ cup dried Cranberries
Fresh Thyme to your liking
1 tbsp Butter

Optional:

Shredded cheese blend

Directions

Cut your biscuits in quarter size. In a large mixing bowl, add biscuit quarters.

Cut orange in half and squeeze out all the juice. Add ½ cup of dried cranberries and sprigs of thyme to your liking. Mix well.

Note: Thyme has a very strong and distinct taste. I used about 4 sprigs.

Layer in bundt pan. Place pan on trivet rack. Add one cup of water to the pressure cooker. Lower pan and trivet into the pot.

Set pot to Manual High Pressure for 35 minutes. Quick release when finished and let cool.

Get ready to pull apart and enjoy! Adding shredded cheese blend is a tasty option or drizzle with a glaze!

Optional Glaze Topping: Over medium heat, melt butter, vanilla and brown sugar.

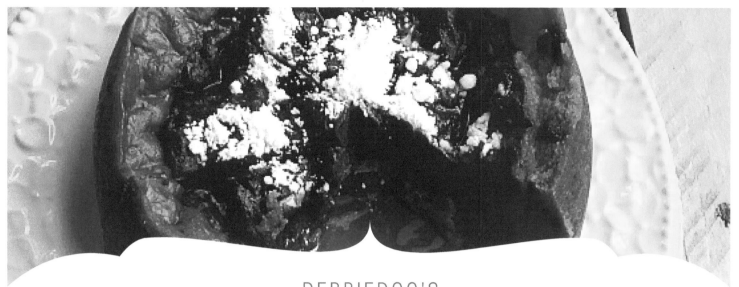

DEBBIEDOO'S
Crownie
Cookie + Brownie!

Ingredients

Cookie dough
(homemade or store
bought)
Brownie mix of your choice
1½ cup water
Parchment paper
Non-stick cooking spray

Directions

Lightly spray the bottom of your spring form pan. Set parchment paper in the bottom round of pan and lightly spray again, also getting the sides of your pan.

Mix brownie according to the box and set aside.

To create your crust, press the cookie dough on the bottom and form to the sides of the pan as well. This creates your crown or bowl-like crust. Make sure to pat and spread evenly and not too thick.

Pour half the brownie mix inside your formed crown. Place pan on a trivet or homemade foil sleeve for ease of getting in and out of pot.

Pour 1½ cup of water in pot. Place your crownie in the pot and set on High Pressure Manual for 75 minutes.

Let natural release. Remove from pot and let set for at least an hour before serving. Yum!

DEBBIEDOO'S
Lemon Supreme Cake

Ingredients

1 box Duncan Hines Lemon
Supreme Cake
3 Eggs
1 cup Water
⅓ cup Vegetable oil
1 can Crushed Pineapple

Optional:
Maraschino cherries

Directions

Mix cake according to box directions. I hand mixed using a whisk.

Prepare 7 inch spring form pan, using the flat portion or bundt portion. Spray pan lightly with a non-stick cooking spray.

Pour entire batter inside pan. Set pan on a trivet. Add one cup of water to the pot. Insert cake in pot. Set on High Pressure Manual for 35 minutes.

Quick release and remove cake. Poke holes on top with a straw and pour the juices from the crushed pineapple can. Let cool for 15 minutes.

Flip cake if you used the bundt portion. Sprinkle with powdered sugar, add crushed pineapple to the center hole and top with cherries. Enjoy!

Peanut Clusters

Ingredients

2½ cups Dry roasted peanuts
(unsalted)
1 lb Melting chocolate bark
3 cups Water

Note:

You will need either a Pyrex plate that will sit resting on top of pot opening or a glass bowl on a trivet in the inner pot liner.

Directions

Pour 3 cups of water into the Instant Pot. Set to saute high. Place Pyrex plate on top of the pot. Add chocolate. This will take about 10 minutes before it starts melting.

Once melting, stir consistently, being sure all chocolate is melted. Set pot on warm.

In a separate bowl, add peanuts and pour chocolate over top. Mix well.

On parchment paper, dollop clusters until all gone. This should make approximately 32 pieces.

Let clusters completely set. You can remove from parchment paper after they have set and place in the refrigerator to cool. Enjoy!

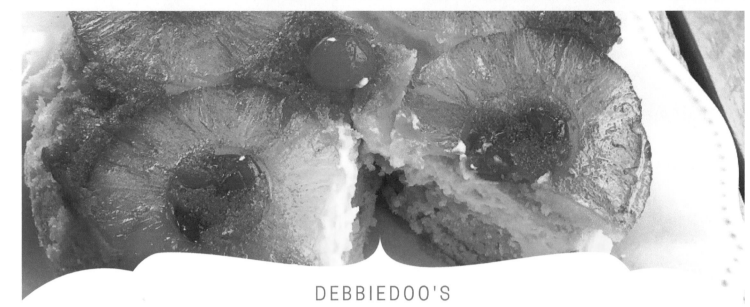

Pineapple Cream Cheese Upside Down Cake

Ingredients

1 Yellow box cake mix
(Duncan Hines preferably)
1 Lemon Jell-O packet
18 oz Philadelphia Cream
Cheese, room temperature
½ cup packed Brown sugar
¼ melted Butter
4 Dole Pineapple rings,
drained
8 Maraschino cherries
3 eggs

Directions

Prepare a 7 inch spring form pan with light cooking spray on the bottom and sides. Add packed brown sugar and butter to the pan. Lightly mix and pat down in pan.

Add pineapple rings and place two Maraschino cherries in the center of each ring. Set pan aside.

In a mixing bowl, add cream cheese, 1 egg and Jello-O packet. Using an electric mixer, mix for about 2 minutes. Set aside.

Mix cake according to box. (I used one less egg than the mix called for.) Add half of cake batter on top of brown sugar and pineapple in pan. Spread evenly.

Add cream cheese and Jell-O mixture, spreading thin and evenly. Pour remaining cake batter on top. Spread evenly.

Add one cup of water to pot. Place pan in pot and set to High Pressure Manual for 55 minutes. Quick release and let cool. Release spring form and using a plate, flip cake over gently. Enjoy!

Pumpkin Bread Pudding

Ingredients

1 box Duncan Hines Decadent
Carrot cake mix
15 oz Pumpkin Puree

Optional:
Walnuts
Confectionery Sugar

Directions

In a large mixing bowl, mix your cake mix and one can of pumpkin puree. Included in the Duncan Hines mix is a carrot and raisin pack. Mix that accordingly and set for 5 minutes. Add it to the mix and stir well by hand.

Spray your cake pan with non-stick spray. Wrap the outer bottom of the pan with tin foil, as the pumpkin puree will leak a tad.

Add mix evenly to the pan and spread out.

Add one cup of water to the pot. Set cake on a trivet rack and lower into the pot. Set pot on High Pressure Manual for 45 minutes. Let natural release.

Let cool and release from pan. Serve in slices, warm with ice cream, a chocolate drizzle or in bite-size pieces with walnuts and confectionery sugar on top. Enjoy!

Pumpkin Cheesecake

Ingredients

2 packages, 8 oz each cream
cheese, softened
¾ cup firmly packed light
brown sugar
3 eggs
15 oz pumpkin puree
1 tbsp flour
2 tsp Pure Vanilla Extract
1½ tsp Pumpkin Pie Spice

Crust:

2 cups vanilla wafer crumbs
3 tbsp butter, melted
2 tbsp granulated sugar

Directions

Prepare crust in 7 inch spring form pan. Lightly spray the bottom of pan. Add the wafer crumbs, melted butter and sugar and mix well to form on the bottom. Place pan in the freezer while preparing the cheesecake mixture.

For the filling, beat cream cheese and brown sugar in a large bowl with electric mixer on medium speed until fluffy. Add eggs, one at a time, beating on low speed after each addition, just until blended. Add pumpkin, flour, vanilla and pumpkin pie spice. Beat until smooth.

Pour mixture over crust in prepared pan and place the pan on a trivet. Add a cup and a half of water to the pot. Lower pan and trivet in pot.

Set pot to High Pressure Manual for 35-40 minutes. Let pot natural release. Gently remove cheesecake and trivet and set to cool. Place in refrigerator for 4 hours to let completely set until ready to serve. Enjoy!

Spiced Pear & Cranberry Cake

Ingredients

1 White cake mix
3 eggs
1 cup Pear juice
15.5 oz can of Pears
½ cup Cranberries
1 tsp ground Cloves
⅓ cup Vegetable oil
½ cup Water

Directions

In a large mixing bowl, mix white cake mix, 3 eggs, 1 cup of pear juice, ½ cup of water, ⅓ cup of vegetable oil, ½ cup of cranberries and 1 teaspoon of ground cloves. Mix well

Note: You may substitute allspice for cloves.

Add 1 cup of water to the pressure cooker. Place cake on trivet or homemade foil sleeve. Lower pan into the pot. Set to High Pressure Manual for 31 minutes. Quick release and let cake cool on a plate.

Once cooled, flip cake over. Add pear slices and a little more cranberry topping. Any remaining pear juice can be drizzled on top. Enjoy!

Weight Watchers Friendly DEBBIEDOO'S

Upside Down Apple Pie

Ingredients

6 Apples

Ground Cinnamon to your liking

Ground Allspice to your liking

Graham cracker crust

1 tsp Butter

5 Caramel candy bites or caramel sauce for topping

Directions

Spray bottom of pan with non-stick cooking spray. In pan, prepare your crust accordingly. I used 4 teaspoons of butter and 1 cup of graham cracker crumbs. Pat down and spread evenly. Place pan in freezer while you prepare the apple mixture.

Slice 6 apples either by hand or peeler. You want them on the thinner side. In a large bowl, combine apples and spices to your own taste. I used approximately 2 teaspoons of cinnamon and a dash of allspice. Mix well.

Remove pan from freezer and add your apple mixture to pan evenly. Add caramel pieces on top. Add 1 cup of water to the pressure cooker. Set pan on a trivet and place in pot. Set to High Pressure Manual for 7 minutes. Quick release and remove from pot. Enjoy!

Optional: Place under broiler for a caramelized top!

This pie has approximately 5 Weight Watchers points per serving!

Pumpkin Banana Cake

Ingredients

1 ripe Banana
2 cups Pumpkin Puree
⅓ cup water
1 yellow Duncan Hines
Cake mix
Dash of Cinnamon

Optional:
¼ cup Chocolate chips

Directions

In a large mixing bowl, add pumpkin puree, banana and a sprinkle of cinnamon. First, hand mix and break up the banana well. Then, beat with an electric mixer for at least 2 minutes. Add in 1/3 cup of water and 1/4 chocolate chips (optional). Add cake mix and mix all together.

Prepare 7 inch bundt pan with nonstick cooking spray. Add 1 cup of water to your Pressure cooker. Add mix to your pan, being sure to spread evenly. Batter is thicker than usual.

Place cake pan on top of trivet and place in pot. Set to High Pressure manual for 35 minutes. Quick release.

Remove cake out of pot and let cool for 10 minutes before releasing spring form. Let cool an additional 15-20 minutes and flip cake over. Enjoy guilt-free.

This pie has approximately 5 Weight Watchers points per serving!

Connect with Debbiedoo

I honestly do not know what I have done for the past few years without owning a pressure cooker. Eating foods that are pressure cooked offers more nutritional boost than those cooked for longer periods using traditional cookware. The longer foods are cooked, the more nutrients are destroyed. I know the older we get, the more nutrients our bodies need. Heck, that goes for our growing children and grandchildren as well. It just makes sense. Pressure cooking is far more efficient than using multiple pots on separate burners, and can result in significant energy savings. Who doesn't want to save money in our energy bills?

Let me mention one more thing that has made my life happier. Cooking with regular stovetop pots tends to leave cooking residues on the stove top and control panel, as well on adjacent surfaces such as walls and counters. Steam and oils escape from open cookware to settle on these surfaces, which usually requires some cleanup after the meal is cooked. A pressure cooker, however, has a well secured lid that prevents any splashes or spatters from escaping the cooking vessel. This also eliminates any boil overs which require further cleanup. And when meal preparation is complete, there's only one pot to wash. Clearly, I will have way too much time on my hands.

For more tips and tricks of the pot, head on over and join our Home Pressure Cooking community. You can find me cooking and testing out new recipes on the blog, check out my favorite cooking essentials at the store, and get in touch with me and the rest of us Home Pressure Cookers over in our Facebook group. We would love for you to join us!

www.HomePressureCooking.com	Blog
www.HomePressureCooking.com/Store	Store
www.HomePressureCooking.com/FB	Facebook Group

CPSIA information can be obtained
at www.ICGtesting.com
Printed in the USA
LVHW072319100220
646419LV00003B/64